NATIONAL GEOGRAPHIC

I Like Apples

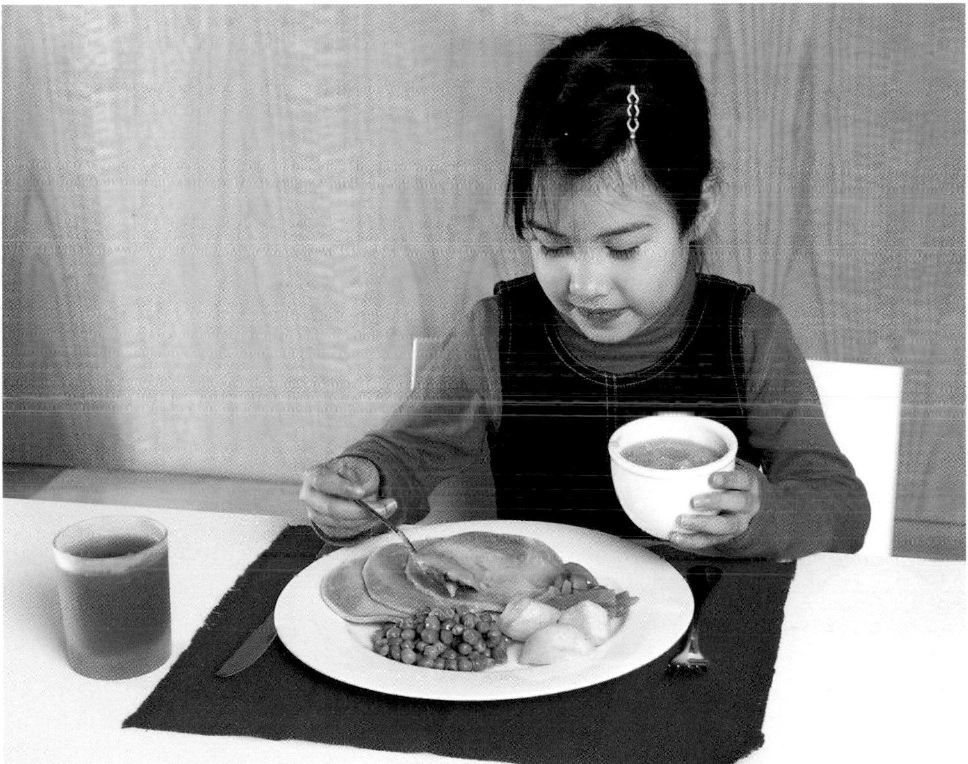

Karl Jense

I like apples.

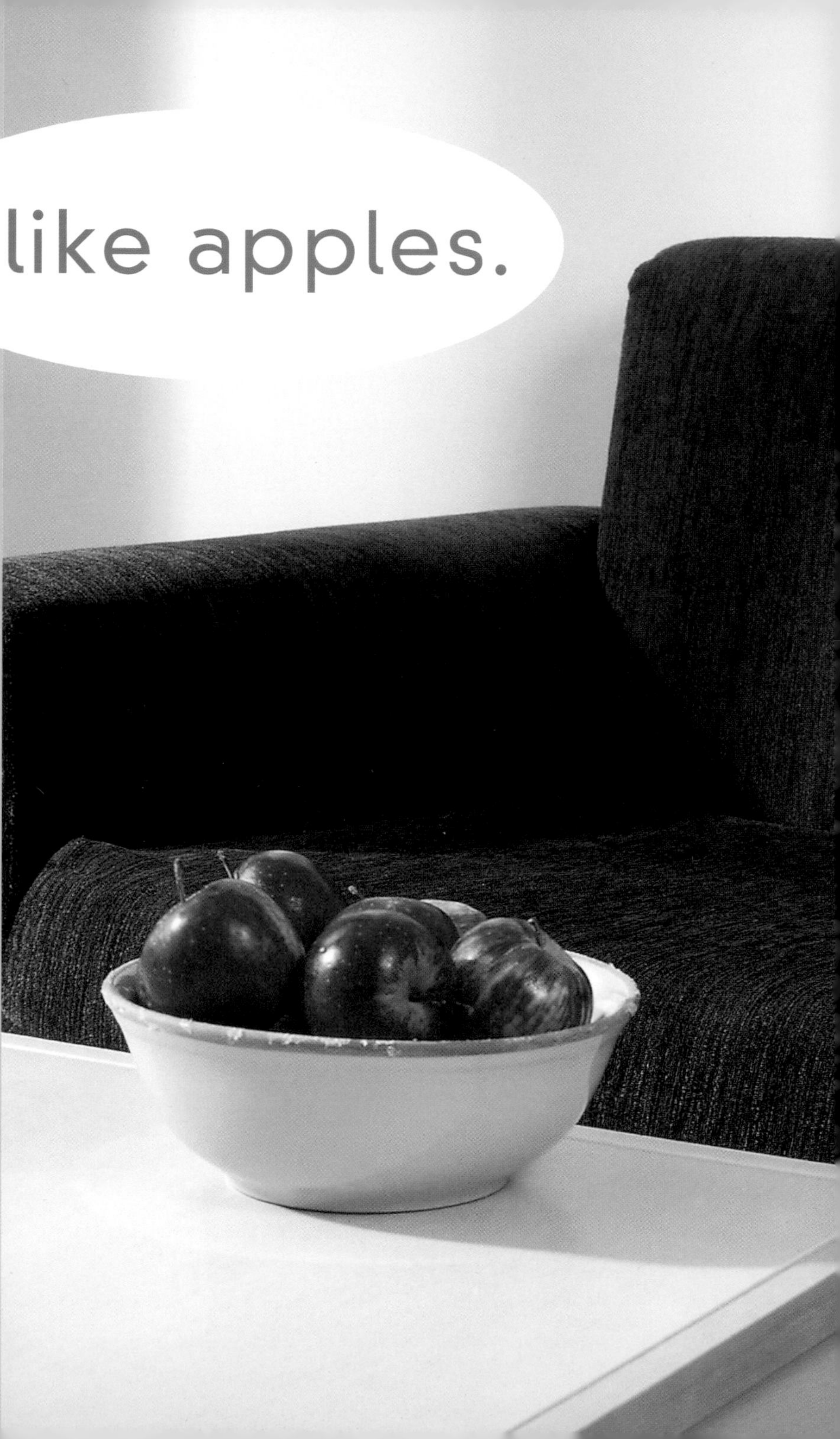

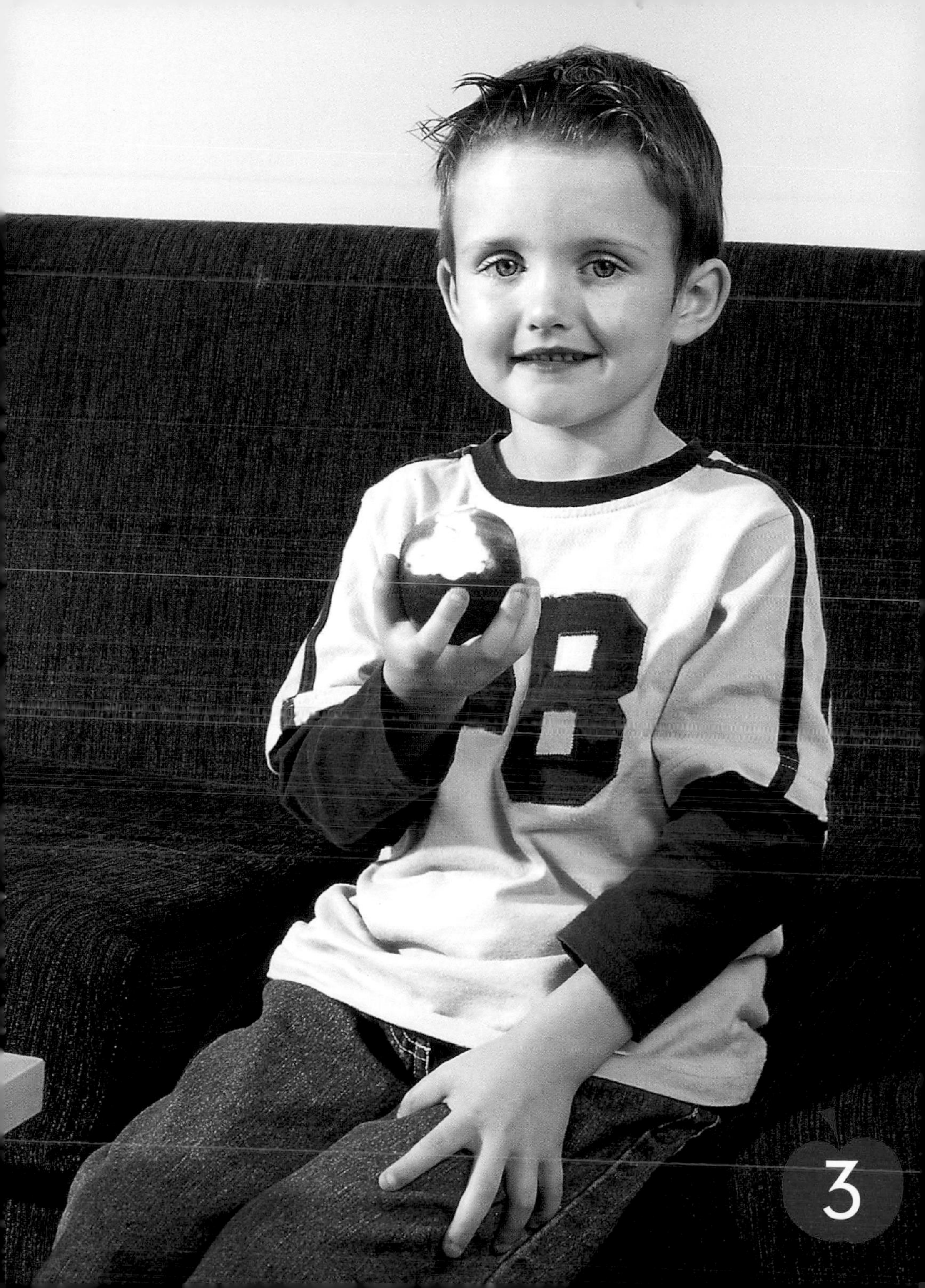

I like apples.

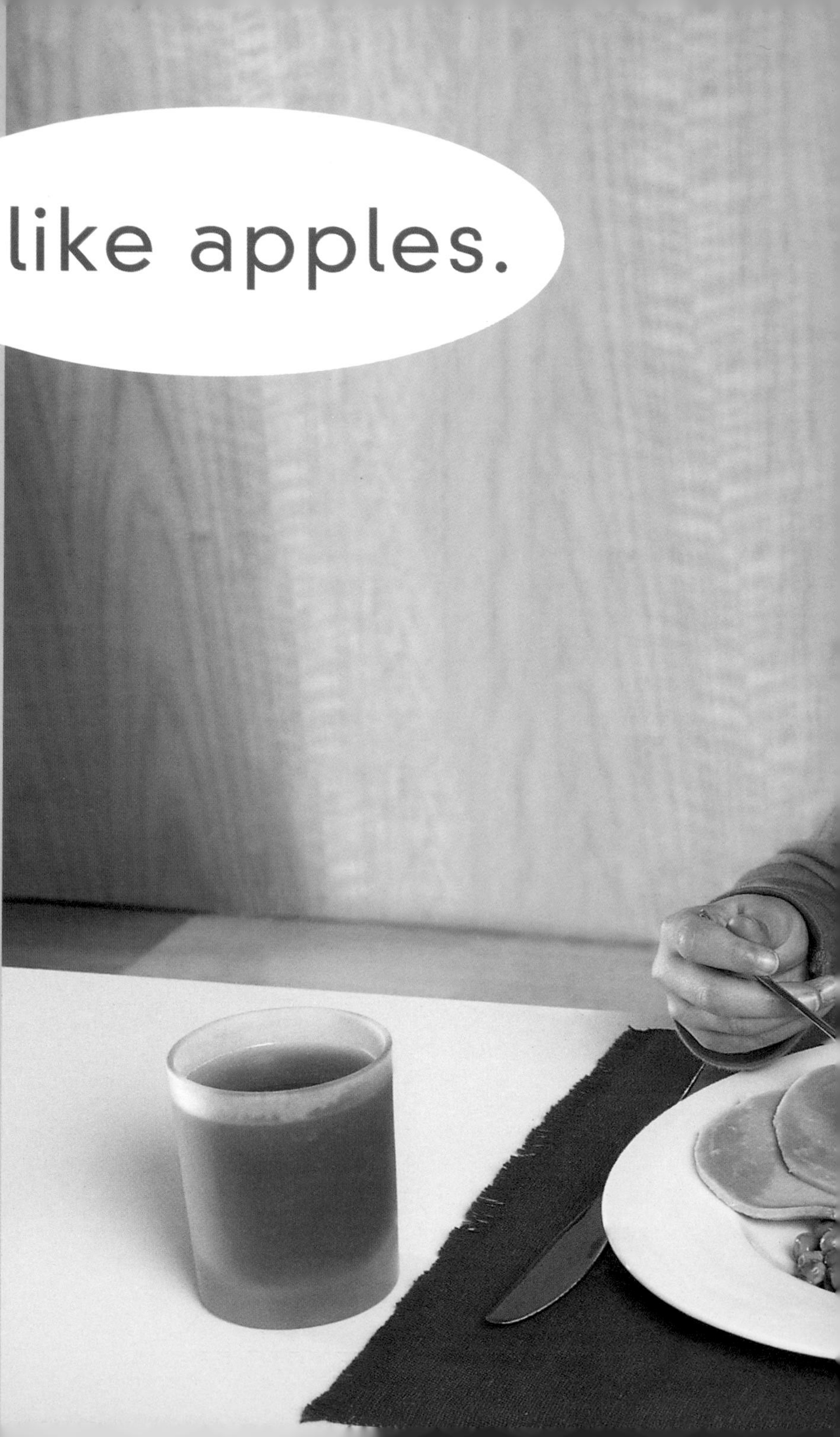

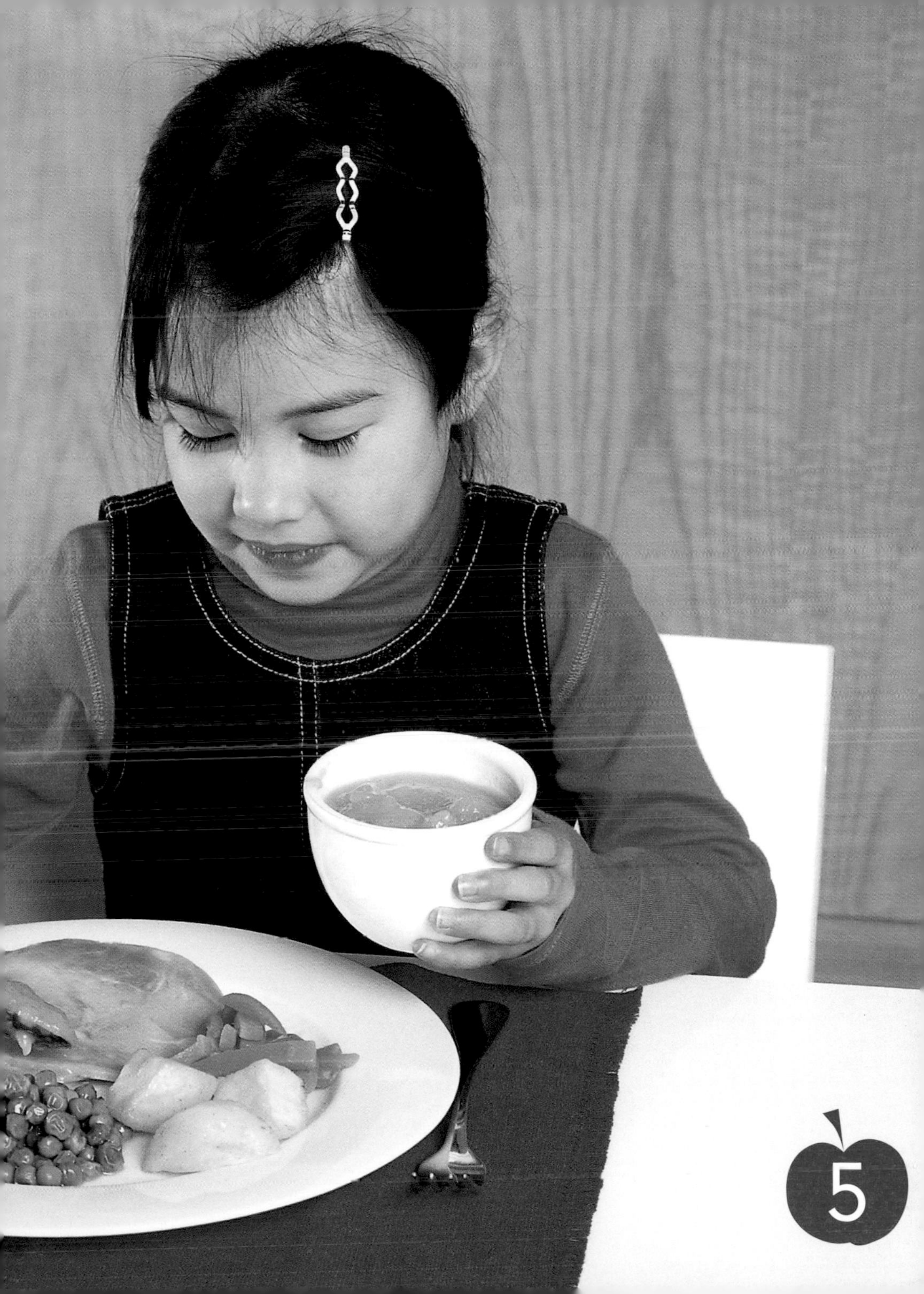

I like apples.

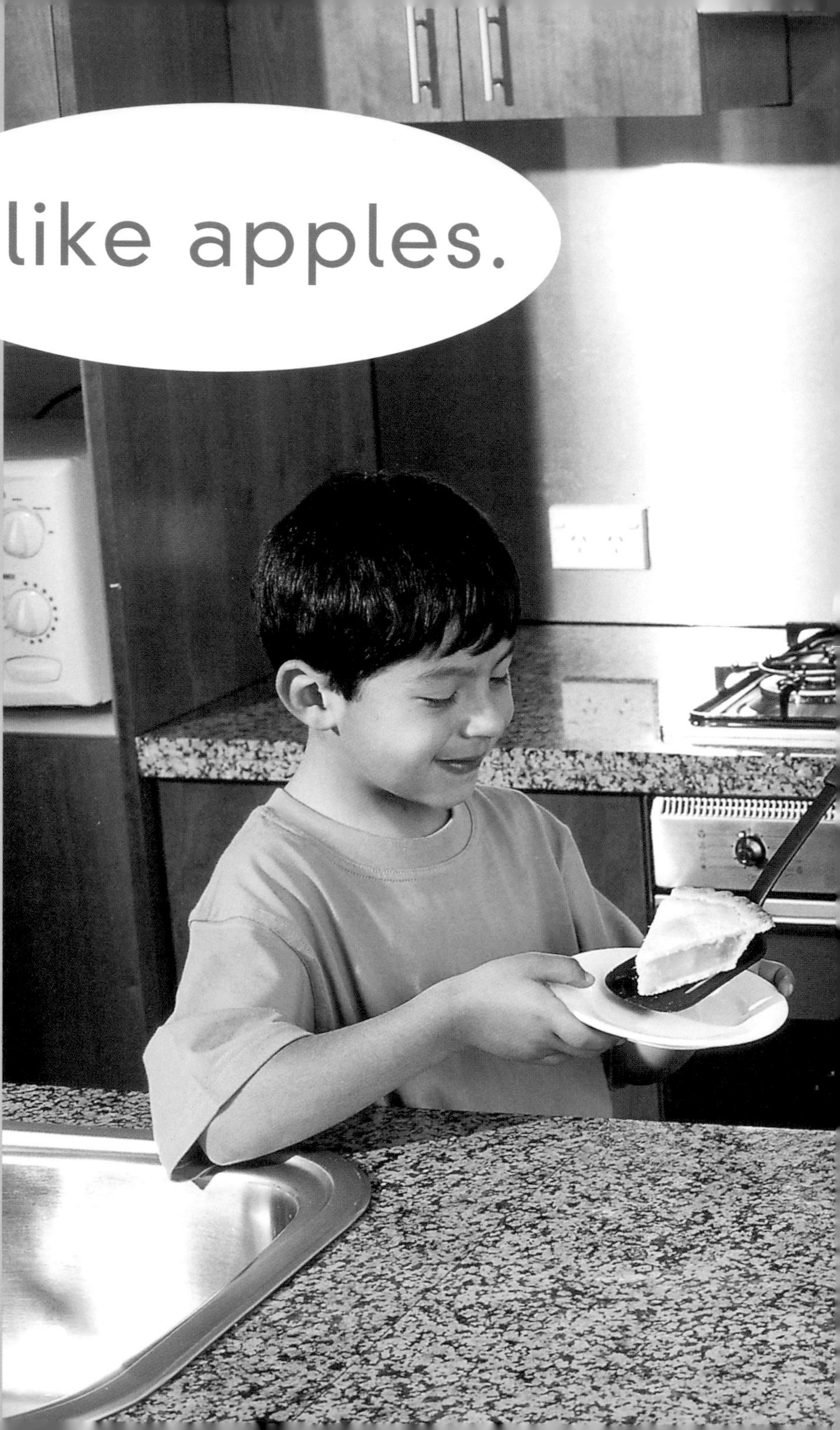

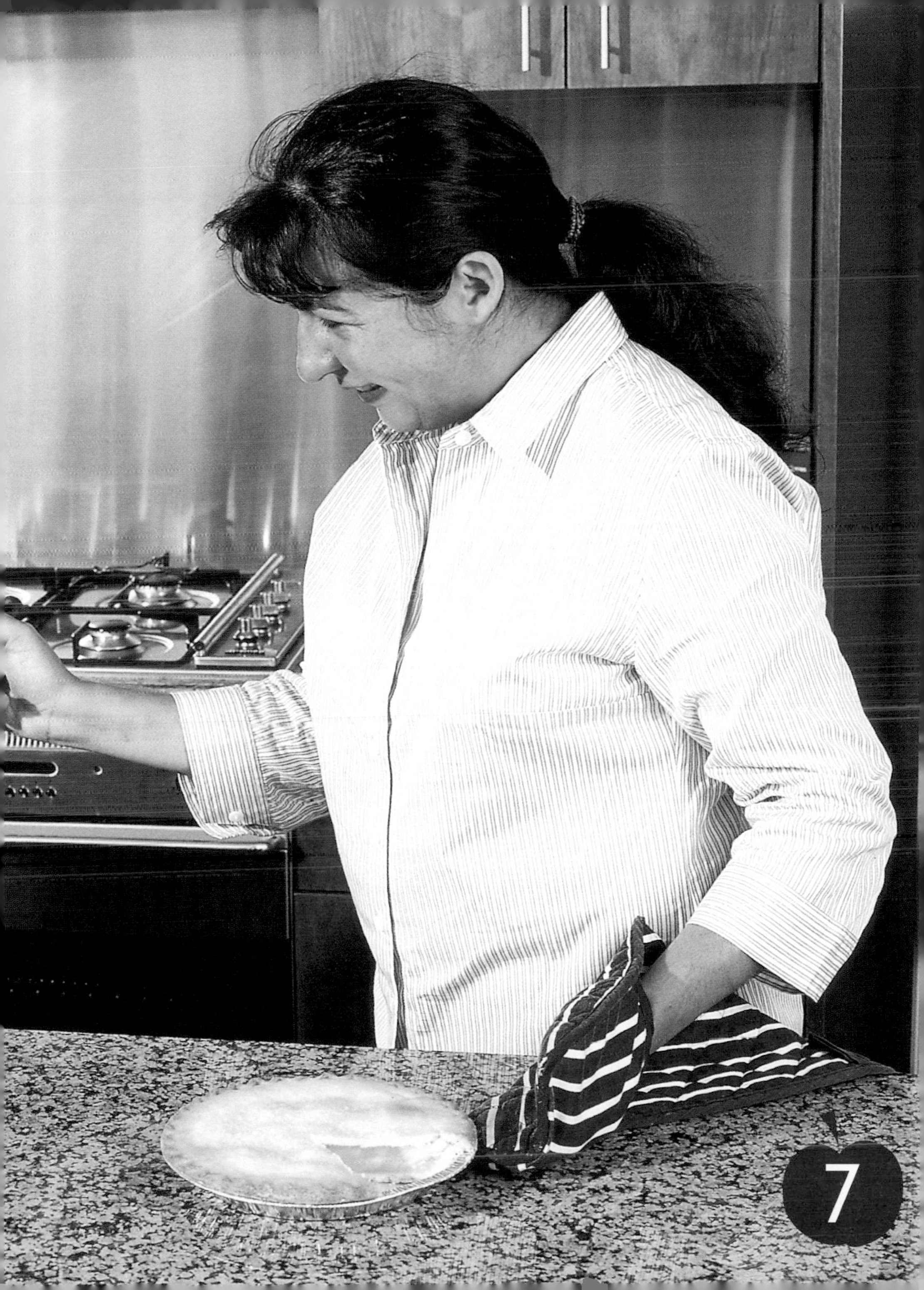

I like apples.

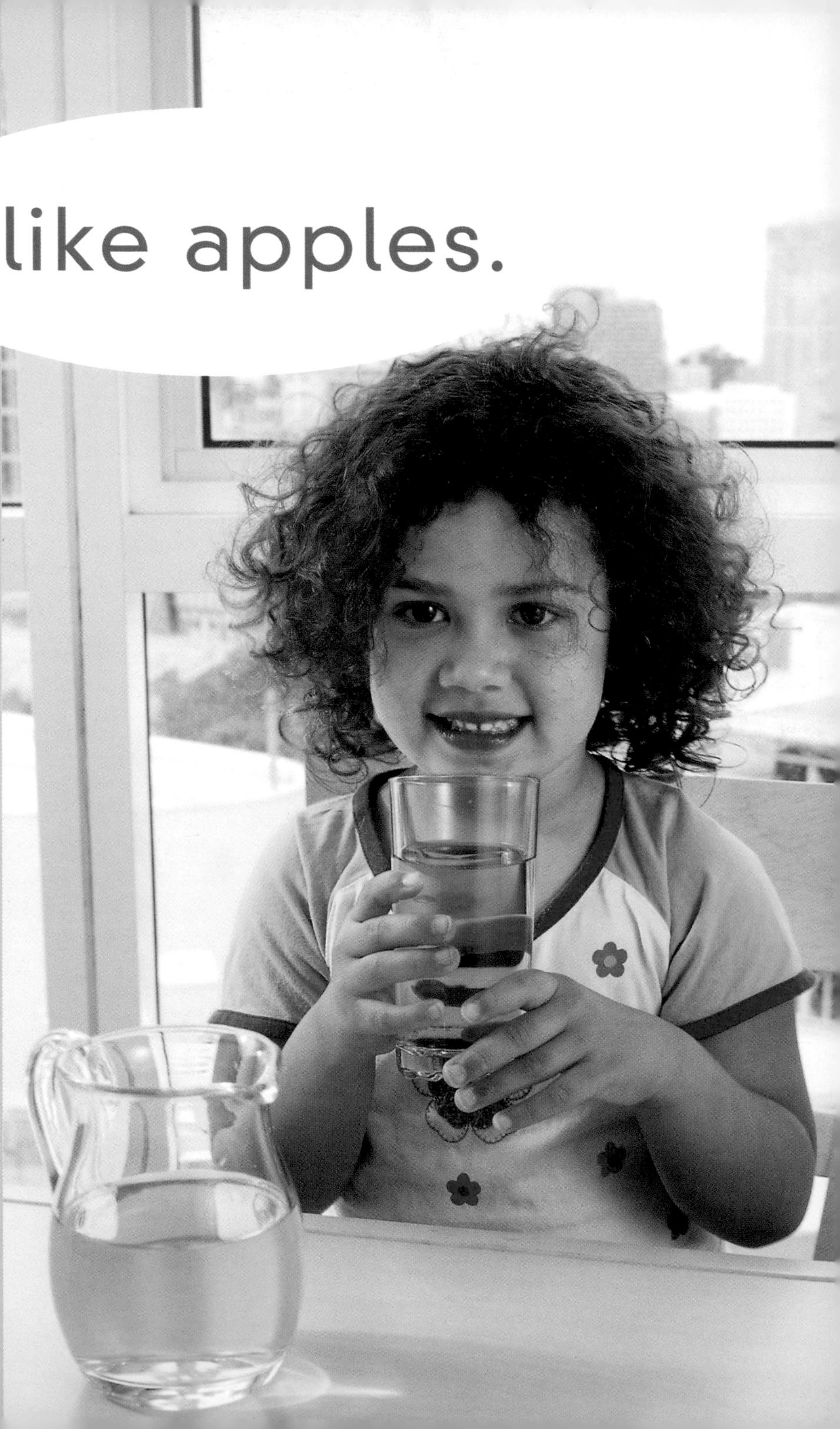